Sort of Gone

Sort of Gone

Poems by Sarah Freligh

Turning Point Books

Published by Turning Point Books
P.O. Box 541106
Cincinnati, OH 45254-1106

ISBN: 9781933456997
LCCN: 2007910199

Poetry Editor: Kevin Walzer
Business Editor: Lori Jareo

Visit us on the web at www.turningpointbooks.com

Acknowledgments

Grateful acknowledgment is made to the editors of the following publications in which these works or earlier versions of them previously appeared:

Aethlon: The Journal of Sport Literature : "Lesson";

The Comstock Review: "Bonus Baby," "Groupie";

Elysian Fields Quarterly: "Minor League," "No-Hitter Fifth Inning," "No-Hitter Seventh Inning," "No-Hitter Ninth Inning," "Spring Training";

Poetry Motel: "Home and Away";

Slipstream: "Novena";

Sport Literate: "Scouting Report."

Poems in this book were previously published as a chapbook, *Bonus Baby*, by Polo Grounds Press in 2002.

"Novena" was nominated for a Pushcart Prize XXVIII.

Thanks to the Constance Saltonstall Foundation for a grant that gave me both the time and inspiration to write many of these poems. Thanks also to my family, to my critique partner, Darby Knox, for friendship and support, and to Thom Ward, for his editor's eye.

These are for Jean Lok Freligh, 1923-1999.

Table of Contents

Buffalo

No-Hitter, Fifth Inning...11
Lesson 12
Yankees..13
Buffalo...14
Eric Moulton, Dead at Eleven..............................15
The Wages of Sin in Western New York.............17
Star...19
Chin Music..20
Night Game...21
MVP: City Championship.....................................22
Home and Away..23
Snapshot: Tomas and Evvie, April 23, 1949........24
Tupperware Party..26

Bonus Baby

No-Hitter, Third Inning...31
Bonus Baby..32
Scouting Report..33
Minor League..34
Groupie...35
Foreign Affairs..37
Sort of Gone 38
Postcard..39

The Show

No-Hitter, Seventh Inning......................................43
Fenway..44
An Old Ballplayer Lectures a Rookie on Girls....45
Al's Answer...47
Rookie Card...48
Relief..50
For Luck...51
Milwaukee Airport, 4:55 A.M................................52
Somonka...53

Sort of Gone

No-Hitter, Ninth Inning..57
Boonie Holds Forth to the Press on Al's
    No-Hitter..58
Spring Training, Thirteenth Season.....................60
Anatomy..61
Pecker Checker..62
St. Francis on Main Street 64
Novena...65
Spring Training, Seventeenth Season...................66
Your Life Until Now..67
Hamlet in the American League............................69
Rehab...71
Al in the Twilight Zone...74
After Seventeen Years, the End.............................75
Dead Men Making Trouble....................................77
Yes, I Have..78
The Math..80
North of Saginaw 81
City of Tonawanda Softball Championship.........82
Nightcap...85

Buffalo

No-Hitter, Fifth Inning

Too early to hope   hell
he's been here before   jinxed
himself by thinking
too much   hung
a curve to some jive rook
who gave it a ride   high
fived his way around the bases

Lesson

For Christmas, Al gets a pitcher's
glove from his old man, real leather
smelling like the inside of a new car
or shoes just out of the box.

Time you learned something,
his father says, finishing off
his first pint of the day,
Adam's apple bouncing

like a ground ball on a gravel
infield. Before dinner they play
catch in the street, shin-deep
in snow. No coats. *We ain't girls,*

his father says, *though you throw like one,*
walks back to where Al is, slaps
him across the face with his callused
hand, says *Son, that's how the ball*
should sound when it hits the glove.

Yankees

They leave early, still dark. Tomas drives, sipping whiskey
from the fifth he's tucked between his thighs. Al props his mitt
against the window to pillow his head, dreams of catching a fly
ball hit by Maris, or better yet Mantle, dreams of leaning over
the railing after the game, one of a flock of boys waving slips
of paper, tickets, programs, chirping *Mick, hey, Mick over here,*
and only Al will have a game ball, gleaming moonbig in his glove
. . . *Albany,* his dad says, snapping the silence of the miles behind
them. The sun comes up, a peacock of light flashing tail
feathers. Al buries his face in his mitt, breathes its shoe-polish
smell, hears his mother laughing at his father's fresh-combed
hair. *Greasy,* she says. *Don't you know a little dab'll do ya?*

Buffalo

Tomas had read about buffalo,
how a storm of them could fill
the prairie, thunder raining
dust that darkened the sky for miles.

On the boat to America, Tomas
practiced walking like a cowboy,
crotch-sprung, saddle-bent from years
of riding the range. *West, buffalo*

he said in English when they stamped
his visa, directed him to a train
that traveled north through canyons
of snow. *Yes, Buffalo,* the conductor

said, pointing to the white humps
of cars lining the sleeping street.
Yes, Buffalo, the punch line to a joke
Tomas sometimes tells himself.

Eric Moulton, Dead at Eleven

Nicknamed the Worm for his thin
skin, pink and raw, his mother covered
with sunscreen before a game, checked
his neck between innings. A real

weird kid, the Worm, bet Al
five bucks that girls had a hamburger
down there a guy could eat, snatched
a hot magazine from the rack at the 7-11

just to get his dough. The Worm
in a closed casket now, blanketed
with roses red as sunburn, red
as blood. The priest tilts

his face toward heaven and says
what a good son he was, good
brother, good grades, good
God, *let us pray for the soul*

of Eric Moulton , dead at eleven.
The family leans into his words
while Al sits with the team,
neat in their green uniforms, watches

the sun boil up dust in the window,
stain the linoleum in scarlet spots,
thinks of his grandmother, dead
to the world after Sunday

dinner, eyes closed, hands folded
over the bell of her stomach
beneath the anguished eye
of a bleeding Jesus. Blood

is why the Worm's casket is shut.
Blew his brains to smithereens but
being a good kid left a note apologizing
for the mess he was about to make.

The Wages of Sin in Western New York

Fourth of July a tornado crashes
parties, backyard picnics, tosses ten
houses a dozen miles north, plants them
in a farmer's field. A warning

God's running out of patience,
says the parish priest, prompting
a parade of people to drive out after mass
to witness just what He has wrought.

Al finds a pair of sneakers that exactly
fit his feet, a catcher's mitt, nearly new,
a birthday card signed Marge and Greg,
a baby doll without its head. Wonders

what Marge did, or Greg, to piss off God,
make Him stir the air with His index finger,
twist the wind so it blew their lives
to kingdom come. What could He

do now to Al, his family, snug in their Chevy,
a blue bead in the rosary of cars strung
bumper to bumper in both directions,
do to them when they bend

to say grace over Sunday dinner?
Suppose there's a heavenly blackboard
somewhere bearing their names, a blizzard
of chalk marks tallied by angels

waiting to give the high sign to Him
that they've run out of chances, time
for a natural disaster to show who's boss.
Afterward would some small boy sift

through the rubble, think about
the wages of sin? Or would he test
the leather of a catcher's mitt, think
finder's keepers, loser's weepers?

Star

Al's stalled in line this far
from where The Mick sits
signing bits of paper and Gleem
white baseballs *to Joey and to Bobby best wishes*
impatiently waits in front of a trophy case
a galaxy of tarnished men trapped
in orbit around photos of Eugene Staniskowski,
twelve-letter man, here,
basketball shorts framing
skinny legs frozen at the apex
of the jump shot that won
a state championship for Buffalo High,
and there, captured
for eternity at the top of his windup. Al
holds the baseball split-fingered
the way Coach showed him, wonders
if his fastball is faster than Eugene Staniskowski's
when he struck out eighteen in the city
championship. Signed by the Dodgers
that year but went with Uncle Sam
instead, and there's the Purple Heart he won
for dying on an island that wasn't
on any map and here's
Mickey Mantle
finally
smaller than Al imagined a hero should be.

Chin Music

My old man's waiting for me after school. *Grab your glove*, he says.
Tells the old lady we're off to the park to play catch. We toss
the ball for ten minutes, then he yanks a handkerchief from his
pants pocket and quits. *You're too much for me today, tiger,* pretends to
mop sweat from his brow. From there it's five blocks to Fred
& Eddie's, enough time to get the spring back in his step, a high
flush to his cheeks, the stud of East Buffalo. When he walks
through the door it's like Jesus Christ himself's come down from
heaven—*Tom, hey, Tom*—the one-eyed man sipping beer
from a wine glass, the woman spilling tits from a leopard dress
as she leans to dig a maraschino cherry from a jar. The old man
drinks the first beer slow, pretending he doesn't need it, then
a second and a third and another and another, lays a twenty
on the bar to *buy the round a house!* deep into his curled-lip, swivel-hip
Elvis imitation for the leopard lady when I slide off the bar stool
and out the door, surprised it's still light. I warm up with a few
throws at the Hires sign painted on the brick side of the bar
then let loose with the good stuff, aiming at the first "o" in root
beer. Again. Again. Faster and harder, until I get the sound right,
the right sound. A watermelon shattering. A skull splintering. High
cheese. Good heat. *You Ain't . . . Nothing . . . But A . . . Hound Dog*

Night Game

Al crouches in the tent his knees
have made of the sheet, transistor
radio tuned to the Yankees, Mel Allen
stabbed by forks of static,

maybe a storm along the line
upstate. Two down, two on
in the ninth when Mantle strides
to the plate to the sound of

his dad shouting, his mom crying
that dinner's ruined again *damn
you* pan smashing *Fuck dinner.*
Ice crashing into glass, breaking

*ball, strike one. Mantle calls time,
backs out of the box, steps in again*
The windup, the pitch on the way,
fouled off into the upper deck, strike two

and fuck you, a door slams and his dad is
*outta here! They're on their feet in Yankee Stadium.
Mic-key Mantle! MIC-Key MAN-tle!
MIC-KEY MANTLE.*

Al punches his glove, imagines
blowing the ball by Mantle hard
into the catcher's mitt. The sound
it would make, like skin on skin.

MVP: City Championship

God,
you want it, yeah, you want it
so bad, you'd trade all you own
for that trophy, your bike, your bed,
your color TV, you'd sleep with a sheet
on the bare wood floor if they engraved
your name on that trophy and yeah, you'd take it
everywhere, carry it with you when you board the bus,
excuse yourself past the losers sprawled drunk in the front
seats, past grocery bags parked in the fat laps of women, past
elderly men dreaming of draft beer and pinochle, oh, they'd all know
you're someone, the most valuable player, the most victorious person,
the most valid pitcher, everything the old man said you'd never be,
and yeah, you'd use that trophy like a beacon to hunt him down
in whatever dark bar he's hiding in, feet twined through
the rungs of a stool, ashtray brimming with dead butts
as he lights his sixty-fifth cigarette of the day,
describing his latest scheme for three people
who don't give a damn. You'd hold up
that trophy and say *Dad, you bastard,*
I did it. I
did it.

Home and Away

The old man's away for a while, Al tells his friends or anyone
else who cares to ask. Says it like his father's gone
to the grocery for cigarettes, over to the bowling alley.
Someplace other than where he really is. Al and his mother
visit once a month, three and a half hours on a Greyhound,
a mile walk up a hill to the place where they wait on a bench
in the sun for his dad to shuffle out in wing tips with no laces
wearing a bathrobe smelling of bleach and old vomit, hands
shaking so bad he can barely get his cigarette lit. *Food's good,*
he says. *How you been?* Al's mother looks at her watch. *Fine,*
Al says, tries to hug the old man when it's time to go

home, after dark, the living room filled up with the day's heat.
Al opens windows while his mother yanks off her stockings,
pours herself a Scotch, settles into the easy chair by the front
window. *Lord,* she says finally, like she's getting ready to ask
for something.

Snapshot: Tomas and Evvie, April 23, 1949

Evvie is smiling. Why not? It's Saturday,
sunny and seventy-two, not a cloud
on the horizon behind her.
She's wearing her Sunday hat,
black velvet banding the crown,
forty dollars downtown,
what she earns in a month frying fish.
Three-inch heels, perfume and a garter belt,
stockings that whisper *soft*
as she walks. She feels like a queen.
It's spring. She's nineteen.
She'd like to be in love.

Tomas is smiling. Why not? He's on furlough
from the steel mill, thirsty for release
from a week of brown bag lunches
and *yes, sir.* He's wearing the fedora
he bought for ten cents at the Salvation Army,
cocked low on his forehead, slicing
his face into shadow and light. He's gangster
handsome, the movie star who gets the girl,
the small-waisted one with the ripe
red mouth.

Tomas and Evvie are smiling. Why not?
Arm in arm, cheek to cheek, fresh
from a nickel cruise to Canada
and back where they shared
a cigarette in the stern as they watched
the buildings of the city shrink.
They smile for the photographer
who doesn't need to say cheese, smile

as they walk the streets holding hands,
past a bum rummaging through a garbage bin,
his clanging hunger dim to their ears,
past men on corners, women on stoops.
Evvie is smiling as she removes
her shoes and tiptoes upstairs
to Tomas' room where he skins
the dress from her shoulders, covers
her breasts with his hands, feels
her heart leap to his touch. He reels
it in, nets it for himself.
She turns and sighs *yes*
to him, hooked.

Tomas and Evvie are smiling.
Why? she wonders. Can't remember
the sun, the cloudless sky, the light
off Lake Erie. Just this:
two fools clutching each other
for dear life, grinning like survivors
of a shipwreck. If they'd stood
in the bow of the boat, they would
have seen the rocks, jagged and black,
the V of the prow knifing
through rough water, the slap
of waves against the hull, seen
what was ahead of them, yes,
the endless slap of waves.

Tupperware Party

       Noon when Evvie steps into the shower, filming
the picture window in the living room with a gauze curtain
of steam on which Al prints his name and H-E-L-P,
hoping a stranger happening past on this dead end
street will be stopped by the cold urgency
of the word, rescue him from this fatherless
house, from a mother who's been snatched
by aliens, replaced with a replicant
in sheer stockings, crimson lipstick, busy swish
of dress. *Help me*, she says, hands him chips
and dip for the living room where *Help*
has evaporated.

       One-thirty when women flock
the foyer, perfumed and girdled, high heels pecking
the wood floor, chirping *hello, hello*, they perch
on chairs, the sofa, refuse the brownies Al offers
help themselves to the rum punch while they twitter
on about calories and fat and the game they play
to break the ice: *Girls, write a want
ad selling your spouse*

       Two-thirty when Evvie unveils an array of bowls
and molds, fills a tumbler with lemonade, presses
the magic button in the middle of the lid— *hear the burp?*——winks
the edges with her finger, inverts it without spilling a drop.
For the grand finale—*watch this, girls*—she performs a grande
arabesque on its upright lid to applause from her audience,
proving how strong, how dependable a container can be.

Four-thirty when Evvie sits, shoes off
at the kitchen table, counting the stacks of fives and
tens while a black woman wails from the radio about
bad love gone worse. Divides their lives into small
piles: this for rent, this for heat, this for
food, this for the bus, this for

        sale, she writes, one husband. Drinks
without spilling a drop. Lid
on tight. Sealed off
from his family
Cheap.

Bonus Baby

No-Hitter, Third Inning

So I get to the mound
and there's Al, laughing
into the fingers of his glove.

Patio furniture, he says.

A guy's on, no outs,
Rodriguez is on deck
and Al's giggling like a kid.

Patio furniture.

Go to hell, I say
hand him the ball
and head back to the plate.

Hey, Boo, he shouts. *What's
Irish and sits on your lawn?*

Bonus Baby

The scout who discovered Al grins
over his Al's left shoulder, smiling like a sailor
sighting land after months at sea, land
at last, when—finally!—Al signs, smiling
his Mickey Mantle smile
for the flash of cameras radiating
the room, for his mom and dad sitting
in folding chairs like small gray paper dolls
pasted there for this occasion.

Afterward Al's paraded through the neighborhood,
perched on a bullet-colored convertible
borrowed from Pulaski's lot, bookended
between his parents who wave like new
Miss Americas to three people drinking
from paper bags in front of Fred & Eddie's,
to the VFW where Al shakes hands with his uncles,
hugs his aunts who cry and bury his head
between the boulders of their breasts.
Al's father sips a ginger-ale, wishing
he could sweeten it with a nip
of whiskey while Al's mother arranges
furniture in the living room of the dream
house Al will buy her.

Scouting Report

Today you know how that Italian felt, sighting
the smudge on the horizon he called America,
land of the free, home of the Braves: *This kid*

can't miss. Four fingers of bourbon in a motel
glass, a cigar outside, a toast to your
discovery. Pretend you don't hear

the honeymooners in the next room playing
ball between the sheets, Mel Allen yelling
going, going, gone. Another drink and another now

you're down to where the bottle demands
you examine your life, consider the score.
Ten thousand innings accounted for

amounting to what? Two ex-wives,
a sister you never see, the rumor of a son
someplace in Texas, a winter ache in your

back, suitcase crammed with a mess
of memories. The past's a gray ribbon
unraveling in your rear view mirror,

each mile sadder than the last, so
here's to the future. Two shots left,
a shortstop to scout tomorrow. Enough.

The moon's a curve ball tonight,
got an arc like you've never seen
might fan Orion on three strikes.

Minor League

Al lives with five other guys
and orange shag carpeting
(the color of insanity, Al has heard),
a hole in the living room
wall weeping plaster where
Boonie put his fist through
trying to prove how tough he was
to a girl he picked up at the pool.

Stu, the handyman, comes to fix it, bringing
his complaints: so much rain, so hard
on the missus, her arthritis. Where's
the old Florida, he wants to know—
flamingos, oranges, blue sky, sun—
snow last winter, can you beat that?
Should have seen all them rich orange
growers up in Orlando watching the sky
like they was waiting for a favor from God.

Boonie cast his hand in masking
tape that everyone wrote on
with a felt-tipped pen. *No brain,*
no pain, Al put, signed his name,
finishing the "l" in a happy face.
Practicing.

Groupie

I hang around with ballplayers because I love
baseball, the game, the guys. Ask the other girls,
any of them, they'll tell you the same thing:
we do it for love, not sex. Sure, the wives
hate us, *what sluts*, they whisper, grab onto their men
but hey, they can't watch them twenty-four hours a day.

They would if they could, the wives, watch them all day,
I mean, chain them to their need like a dog. What kind of love
is that, I ask you. They don't understand their men
at all, which is why a ballplayer spends time with a girl
like me, someone he can talk to, but you can't tell the wives
that. They look at me like I'm not a person but a thing

to ignore or avoid, like shit on a sidewalk, something
dirty and I'm not. Last week on San Diego Chicken Day
the Chicken picked me to dance, *me*, not one of the wives
even though they're prettier than I am and God knows I love
to dance. I showed off my moves, got people yelling *You go, girl*,
shook my butt, shimmied my boobs. I got the men

going a little crazy, whistling and stomping their feet. Some man
in the front row stood up, threw money at me, nothing
big, but hey, it was a joke, because I'm not the kind of girl
who does it for money, some whore who screws twenty men a day.
I need a guy to tell me I'm beautiful, tell me he loves
my red toenails, loves how I listen to him, how he wishes his wife

were more like me. Just once I'd like to say to the wives
when they give me the evil eye: *Why don't you ask your old man
where he really was yesterday when he went out for cigarettes.* Loving
me, that's where, three times. I'd tell her all the things
he said to me: how we're going to be together someday
when he gets to The Show, how he should have married a girl

like me instead of the prom queen from high school, the girl
voted most likely to succeed, the girl who's now the wife
who won't listen when he tries to tell her about the bad day
he had at the ballpark. As long as there's women like that, men
will need someone like me to talk to, give him the things
he's not getting at home, pamper him a little. That's true love

isn't it? A girl who's been around as much as I have knows what a man
wants, and it's not a wife who's on him for every little thing
he does. So watch it, sister, or someday he'll be mine to love

Foreign Affairs

In every ballpark, a pair of girls in halter-tops,
breasts displayed like fruit on a tray; tan, spandex skin,
hair a guy could lose himself in. Boonie flips
him for the blond, tails Al gets the brunette. Nothing
to write home about but okay for a night.
He buys her some kind of rum drink, five shots
of booze and juice, topped by a little red kite.
He sips a beer and tries not to stare at her tits
while she tells him she once saw Nolan Ryan
down to the Shell station pumping his own
gas, smaller than he looks on TV. Al practices when
and how he'll say he loves her. Tossed like a bone
to a dog or coins at a tollbooth. The arm lifts, you're in.
This highway's crowded. A gridlock of women.

Sort of Gone

Tommy's locker's bare of everything but
last month's Playmate—Miss May, a string
of pearls threaded through her black bush—
taped where the team can reach up, rub

her boobs for luck. Tommy, who once told
a reporter he sort of believed in extraterrestrials,
believed that Jesus had been an alien—how
else could he walk on water? A rightie

with a lefty's head, said the story. Tommy,
just out of the shower when Skip squinted
through the gloom of steam, asked to see him.
A dozen bare backs turned ignorant out of respect

or fear. Now, looking at Miss May they think
of Tommy, remember how nuts he was,
laugh until their guts ache, forgetting
that one day they'll all be sort of gone.

Postcard

dad, got in the game today,
struck out three, skip says
I'll make the show—al

The Show

No-Hitter, Seventh Inning

Alone at the end of the dugout
Al thinks of fishing, catch
and release, sits
so he can't see the scoreboard
over center field, zeroes
burning the dark.
Seven mouths shouting.

Fenway

Coach used to say you had to know
a ballpark the way an Indian would,
as a living thing, a spirit that enters
you through your toes, surges
up and into your fingers
until you're able to claim it
for your own. Injun Frank,
they called him behind his back,
or Frank the Fag after Coach
got nabbed in a dragnet eyeballing
a magazine full of naked boys
in a store downtown.

Al's just up from Triple-A, fresh off
an all-night drive from Rochester,
zoo breath and stinking, 56 cents
in his pocket and yet
the clubhouse guy calls him sir,
pours him coffee with real cream.
Fenway's a cathedral greener
than money, seats and grass,
the green sky of the Monster rising
from the horizon in left. Sure, the same
ninety feet between bases,
sixty feet from mound to plate, older
than time and still, he makes sure
no one's watching before he kneels
to kiss the grass and claim it
for the country of Al.

An Old Ballplayer Lectures a Rookie on Girls

Think of them as wild
flowers. Weeds. Pick one

from the bunch
blooming by the clubhouse,

a garden of breasts
and legs. Toss her out

in the morning
with yesterday's trash.

Ignore her when she knocks
some night, bringing curtains

for your kitchen window, clean
sheets for your bed.

Tell her you got
no time for no

bodies. Tell her you're
going to be

big, you're going
to be someone, you're

part of The Show.
Years from now

you'll bend
to kiss the bouquet

of your daughter's face
want to kill the bastard that was you.

Al's Answer

"Ain't you got no heart, boy?"
—Dino DiMino, Al's pitching coach

There. It's there, he knows, just below his right
hand *I pledge allegiance to the flag*
there under skin and bone, caged tight
in the prison of his ribs, a heavy bag
of muscle, a ham-pink fist punching away
in his chest, a heavyweight contender *under*
God indivisible, no quit in this baby,
none, no way will Al Stepansky ever
give up. He'll go the distance, give you
nine innings of flat-out goddamn great
ball, wring his guts out, tear his soul in two
trying to show up those rubes at the plate,
goddamn dying to prove he's the best,
a winner, prove to you he's got a heart.

Rookie Card

That kid in the picture—hands tucked
in his glove, frozen at the top
of his windup while the old fart
photographer wheezed and fumbled
to focus the shot. Hurry up, pop, the kid
said. Can't stay this way forever, though
sometimes when his fastball
was cooking, practically sizzling
past the batter, when his curve
fell off the edge of the earth, when his knuckle
ball tickled the wind—he knew he'd
get even God to whiff on three pitches.

The photographer said, *Say cheese*,
and the kid imagined trays of it,
and wine, red and white, on a glass table
in his dream apartment, wall to wall
blonds, a fur rug, maybe a piano though
he didn't play, everything clean and white
the way it never was at home. *Okay,*

said the photographer, who didn't know
that in a month he would pick up
a check the waitress dropped
next to his plate of spaghetti
at a lunch counter near Tampa, put
a hand over his fiery heart and die.
You never know, the waitress
would say to the kid who bought her three

strawberry daiquiris one night and told her
she looked like Marilyn Monroe. Later
the kid watched her turn and sigh
into sleep. He lit a match to study
the ruin of her body: fallen
breasts, ancient thighs, pink scar smiling
up from her belly. The match
burned down, singed his fingers.
God, how long before morning?

Relief

Seeing her you're reminded of the uniform
you left limp and crumpled on the locker
room floor night before last, the eternity
you waited for the stopper
to come out of the bullpen, save you
from a eulogy of boos. The end
you tried to wash away.

Seeing her wrapped in the afghan
she made while you suffered
through the flu, through third grade
arithmetic: 9 times 9
is 81, she said, rock and crochet.
She could have been something:
a scientist, an actress,
a maker of maps, anything
but a girl who fried fish
in a corner bar, married your father.

Seeing her, you realize there's nothing
left, nothing to do but wait for Death
to emerge from the bullpen, begin his slow
showy walk from the outfield to the mound
black satin jacket shrouding his shoulders.
The end, at last, relief.

For Luck

Outside a deli in Chicago a woman wearing
a tutu atop a torn kimono holds out her hand,
demands anything, sir, anything at all. Al
empties his pockets—pennies and dimes—everything

but the loonie a stripper gave him in Montreal
after dancing in his lap. *For luck,* she said. Older
than the other girls but still nice, a damp
warm bundle of woman heating his jeans.

Al went back weeks later, sat through three shows
waiting to tell her the loonie had saved him, saved
his season *You're outta luck, pal,* the bartender said,
gave Al free beer in exchange for his autograph.

The woman tucks Al's change in her kimono,
adjusts her tutu and salutes: *Good luck in the war,
sailor,* lurches toward a liquor store
singing a Puccini aria of love and loss.

The stripper had a French name Al
would whisper when he couldn't sleep:
    Jeanne Marie
       Jeanne Marie
          Jeanne Marie

Milwaukee Airport, 4:55 A.M.

Swimming into the sea
green light of the baggage
claim, coming up for air

the buzzer sounds, signaling
progress, they press forward,
a weary herd heading

for the trough
of suitcases. Al drags his
bag from the carousel

before it orbits
into the dark,
walks to the bus.

The sun is up.
Another city.

Somonka

Postcard
I am writing this
from Houston. Fourteen days now,
out of underwear.
San Fran is really something.
Who wouldn't leave their heart there?

Telegram
Regret to inform
you your mom passed on Tuesday.
Stop. Buried today.
Stop. No need to return home.
Stop. Best to stay where you are.

Sort of Gone

No-Hitter, Ninth Inning

Two down, his hands too big, wider than shovels and heavier,
hanging from his wrists, the windup, the pitch high and outside
Could argue that it nicked the corner, fuck it, walk, spit, breathe,
inoutinoutinoutinout in time to the angel choir singing in his head,
gloria in excelsis deo, Gloria in first grade deo, stuck a blue crayon
in her underpants, made Al pay her a dime to get it back, took
his red crayon too then, Gloria Dombrowski. Supposes Gloria
is a hooker someplace wearing black underpants bulging
with the crayons of businessmen on long lunches, *gloria*
in a whorehouse deo, got away with one there, right down the pipe,
the batter so surprised he lunges at it, too late, tipping it foul
into the upper deck, two strikes now, the batter steps out,
says something to Boonie who nods and laughs, something
about gloria, yeah, in excelsis deo, the batter leaning in
again, gold 21 hanging heavy from his neck, pulling him toward
the plate into strike three swinging and Al is drowning under a tide
of bodies and the tsunami of sound that crashes down on him,
AL! AL! AL! poking staccato holes in heaven through which angels
will fall, *Gloria in excelsis deo . . .*

Nothing, Al says to the reporters who crowd his locker. *I wasn't*
thinking of nothing out there.

Boonie Holds Forth to the Press on Al's No-Hitter

Wherever I put the glove, he hit it.
Fastballs, sliders: He got everything
where it was supposed to be
tonight. It was magic.

Yeah, fastballs, sliders every time,
nothing fancy about it, man.
No magic tricks tonight,
I told him in the third inning,

don't get fancy. Got a man on,
no outs, Rodriguez on deck,
and it's only the third inning.
Then Benton hit that dribbler,

two gone now and Rodriguez up.
A 1-2 count and Al throws a cutter
that Rodriguez dribbles down to first
and Al's out of a jam thanks to

that cut fastball on a 1-2 count.
Fifth inning, it's déjà vu all over again.
Another jam, no thanks to
the ump calling ball on a 3-2 count.

I'm thinking here we go again
and called time to talk to Al, told him
to shake it off: the ump, the bad call
and damn, man, did he ever.

Nope, we haven't talked yet. I'll tell him
he was magic out there tonight,
damn, was he ever. He was *the man*.
Wherever I put the glove, he hit it.

Spring Training, Thirteenth Season

Running wind sprints along the outfield
fence, ten eleven twelve times past
the Ramada sign, painted blond
in a red bikini, *Fuck you, pussy*
scrawled across the hills
of her tits. Al bends to get
his breath back, the smell
of just-cut grass reminding him
of the first time he made love.

Anatomy

Tonight, a toothache
in his shoulder
punching him awake
at 4 a.m. to infomercials
about acne and the heartbreak
of unwanted flab. He chases
five aspirin with a shot of Scotch
watches a blond
open her thighs to him,
say *look,*
how easy it is.

Pecker Checker

You're nearly naked, arm deep
in ice when *she* appears, aims
her tape recorder at your face, starts firing
questions at you like, How did you feel
watching that homer go over
the wall and, How did you feel
when Skip yanked you and on and
on until you feel like snatching
the towel from your lap, saying *feel this,*
pecker checker. But you smile and serve up
the usual crap: *It's just part*
of the game, got to suck it
up, tomorrow's another day
thank God.

For once, why don't you give her
what she wants? Why don't you tell her
how the walk to the dugout seems like
forever, how the boo birds chirp on
in your head long after the game is over
no matter how loud you crank your car
radio, tell her how Doubt and Despair
ride shotgun, remind you what a loser
you are. Tell her how they come home
with you, stomp through your living room,
prop their dirty feet on your white furniture,
pilfer snacks from the refrigerator. Tell her
how they follow you upstairs, climb under
the covers with you and fuck
with your dreams and isn't that

what she needs to hear, what she wants?
You bare-assed for the whole world
to see, yeah, the naked truth.

St. Francis on Main Street

Al walks down a hall paved
with cracked linoleum, littered
with wrecks of men, mumbling,
and tied to wheelchairs,
to the room where his father lies
in piss-stained sheets, wondering
where Al's mother is,
why dinner is late.
In the next bed, a man named Sam
sings Christmas carols
to a sock he rocks like a baby
while Al strokes his father's hand,
coiled in sleep, afraid it will
wake up, strike at any time.

Novena

Late Saturday. The ancient
neighborhood restless

with drunks, amplified rap
trembling windows,

the one-eyed man
chanting his incessant

catechism from the steps
of St. Stanislaus: *Sinners*

burn for eternity. Al kneels
on a crimson cushion, lights

a candle for his mother, another
for his father, a third asking

God to give him
back his fastball, heal

his shoulder please, make
the ache go away *please*

God damn it please. Asks
His forgiveness for asking.

Spring Training, Seventeenth Season

He was walking to the drugstore when it happened. *For a razor
to slit my throat* is what Al tells the cop, who asks him to autograph
his ticket book. *Seven runs in one inning, shit.* Yeah, Al noticed
the blue Chevy. Because of the old man, he supposes, spine
straight in the driver's seat, hands on the steering wheel at 10 and 2,
going real slow, leading a parade of impatience—*C'mon pops,
Step on it, dad*— horns honking, the usual Florida street war.
The old man, head poking from the shell of his starched
white collar, dressed to the nines for the early bird special
at Denny's, probably dreaming of meat loaf when his car rockets
into the intersection, pinballing off a van full of beered-up college
boys into a telephone pole, Al running now, the first
to reach the Chevy. *Harriet,* is all the old man says, eyelids
flickering, dead of a heart attack, according to the paper
the next day. Eighty-three years, summed up in an inch,
while Al's loss gets twenty-four, plus a photo.

Your Life Until Now

A disaster on an eight-lane highway. A ten-car pile-up you've
caused or, if you're lucky, an accident you happen past. You don't
want to look but you do. Admit it—you're fascinated

by the panoramic landscape: Mountains of loss darkening
the horizon, mistakes littering both shoulders of the road,
gray sky raining failure. Fate has driven you this far, or God,

though His son's the one you picture behind the wheel, a lit
cigarette dangling from His lips, chauffeur's cap askew,
Where to, dude? He says, a yellow glow behind Him

like the rim of the world right before the sun cracks
through. Hippie hair and beard, tired eyes turned
heavenward, too weary to continue and still no end to the shit

He must shovel for us sinners: *Dad, can't the Holy Ghost
take the wheel just this once?* He's a good driver, Jesus,
keeps the speed between seventy, seventy-two, rides

the clutch a tad too much for your taste, maybe a little
bit preachy in His insistence that you consider
your sins. He's tuned into salvation, redemption,

wants you to sing along while you'd as soon
doze or study the scenery, anything but dredge up
that old dreck. Miles of silence until you say, How

about those Yankees? *Your dime, your time,*
He says, right wrist cocked over the
steering wheel, gangster lean suggesting

He'll wait an eternity if he has to. That's the Jesus
you know, just another guy soldiering through life,
marching through sorrow and loss like the rest of us

because there's a heaven at the end of the road for everyone
or so God promised. *Only ten more miles, pal. Hang in.*

Hamlet in the American League

Funny, how often he thinks of her,
that long-ago girl who once upon a time
read him the plays of Shakespeare.
Delia, short for Cordelia, a daughter
of Lear, she said, so Al of course
asked for a ride on the old man's
jet sometime. Cordelia wore rings
on every finger, gold hoops that jingled
when she tossed her hair, dressed
in black though Florida was hotter
than Hades in August. Cordelia
scribbled in a notebook
when she wasn't issuing rent
receipts, a play about two kids
in love, a rich boy and a poor girl,
Romeo and Juliet meet *Hamlet*
because she planned to drown
the girl in the rich boy's
swimming pool where he sat all day
drinking gin and lemonades thinking
up ways to kill his father. Al
supposed he loved her if love
was someone who listened
to stories about your old man,
how he hit you now and then
for the hell of it until the day
he dried out. After that, he dried up,
like he was made of paper but all that
is so long ago Al's forgotten
who died first—Romeo or Juliet—forgotten
the speech he once memorized for her
and carried in his head until

the words were crowded out by other
women, other words. Odd how often
he thinks of her now whenever
he's alone on the mound bearing
the whips and scorns of booing,
unruly fans and how at such times
a phrase will break loose from the muck
on the floor of his mind, float
up into the clear water of memory
bright as a knife's blade slicing
the wall between remember and forget:
Good night, sweet prince.
His sword is broken, his troops
in disarray from a barrage
of hits and, oh, to be
that character he played once, Acts II
and III ahead of him, oh, to be
that boy again.

Rehab

Rehabilitation assignment: A period during which a
player is sent to a team playing at a lower level so that
he can reestablish his ability.
—The Dickson Baseball Dictionary

I. Fort Lauderdale

A small brass band playing Sousa, two
        majorettes in gold lame, eight
girls in white boots twirling flags, Ten
Cent Beer Night, cups snatched the instant
        they're filled, a sellout crowd
            for Al Stepansky. 7:17
p.m. when Al walks toward the dugout by third
        base, wearing his age, 39,
    tips his cap at the sound of 20,000
        hands clapping.   Four
men in ties settle into seats three
rows behind home plate. One
        aims a radar gun at Al,
    fixing him in its crosshairs.

II. Alligator Alley

Before the bus has passed the neon hem
        of fast food joints skirting
    Fort Lauderdale, the right fielder
        has locked the shortstop
    in the bathroom, the middle reliever
    has stuffed the first baseman

71

into the overhead rack, the back-up catcher
has opened the fifth of tequila
he bought with a fake ID: Last shot
eats the worm. Puke
and you'll never live it down.

Frayed silver ribbons wave
from a wooden cross, rotted
flowers mark the spot
where someone veered
out of this life and into
the next one, not
far from where Al once paid to see
an Indian kid pin an alligator
to the ground, opening its jaws
to show two rows of teeth,
yellow and deadly.

The Dow Jones up a hundred yesterday climbing
just as a guy in Ohio said, Please
and Thank you to the teller he robbed,
turned and sprayed the room
with bullets killing four,
while in South Dakota more
rain fell, eight inches in an hour,
Who said hell was hot?
In Detroit a man
and his Alzheimer's wife grasped hands,
leaped together from the Ambassador Bridge
and in Fort Lauderdale, a man behind
home plate checked the radar gun,
shook his head, the look of someone
pulling a sheet over the face
of a body, newly dead.

Two down, a five-letter word for
someone who fails
where they once succeeded—
L
O
S
E
R

Al in the Twilight Zone

The guys say hi to him, high five him say
they're glad he's back, don't look him in the eye
though, look instead for that black batting glove
they wear for luck or the bag of chew they think
they opened the day before. Al starts to feel
like that man on TV the other night,
a guy just sprung from the loony bin,
flying home with his wife, minding his own
when he sees this Thing, hairy-hooved and god awful,
banging on the wing but it can't be a monster, no way,
so the guy wakes his wife and tries to tell her
about the Thing, but when she looks there's only rain, lightning,
the plane plowing the night, Honey, you're tired,
take a Milltown, relax, and he tries but he can't
quit thinking about the monster, how he saw
what he saw so he opens the curtain
and there's the Thing at the window, steaming
the glass with its bad dead breath, its smoldering
coal eyes and the guy starts screaming, crying,
until he's wrestled down, shot up, wheeled off
on a stretcher straight back to the funny farm
just as Rod Serling enters, lit cigarette in hand,
tells us we've just traveled through
the Twilight Zone as the camera pans the wing,
the mess of metal, so there, the guy wasn't nuts
after all, and neither is he, god damn it,
so why does he feel like something
terrible is out there watching
what he does every second, waiting
for him to fuck up?

After Seventeen Years, the End

It's like that dream, your nightmare where talk
flattens into static, scrambling words into
nonsense, noise, only this time it's real and still you
can't comprehend words like *sorry, finished, age*, words
if told to pick a partner would have chosen
to stay by themselves on the sidelines, restless hands

jammed deep into their pants pockets. You stand, shake hands
with everyone—Skip, the Boss, his secretary—make small talk
about the weather, *rain today?*, try to act like it was your choice
to walk away and wasn't it? For the good of the club, in order to
free up the money for some young arms? How quickly their words
become yours, a script you rehearse until you

get it right, the complete team player. Too soon it's time for you
to fix your tie, put on your game face, meet the press. More hands
to shake, then it's just you alone in the grill of lights, but the words
you practiced won't come, so you clear your throat and begin to talk
about stuff: How grass smelled after it was just cut, how twice
your rookie year you nearly quit, but instead you chose

to hang in there. Silence, then someone asks: *Is this your choice*
to walk away? You lean into the mike and say you've
had a great run, God willing, but it's time to move on to
other interests. Like what? All this time on your hands
maybe you'll grow roses. Or something. You're sweating, the talk,
the lights, their questions coming at you from the right, the left, words

aimed at you like missiles targeted to get the truth. Finally the words
you've waited for—*Thanks, guys*—the lights dim, it's over. You choose
the back way to avoid the crowd and because all this talk
has made you thirsty. You find a bar that looks as crappy as you
feel, a neon cathedral of beer signs, a shrine to the lost and lonely. You
hand the bartender a fifty for a shot and a beer, order two

more when it occurs to you you're just another barfly staring into
his glass like it's the oracle, sitting in a bar that's silent as a church, a
    wordless
communion of losers. The guy next to you lifts his beer glass with
    shaking hands
and sips, chasing salvation at the bottom of the glass. Another guy
    chooses
a couple songs on the jukebox, no, the same song four times, one you
don't know but you sing along anyway because singing is simpler than
    small talk

and drinking is easiest of all. A high sign to the bartender, the choice
stuff this time, *a round for the house*, words you learned young from
    your
old man. Same hands and face, all hot air and promise. Big man.
    All talk.

Dead Men Making Trouble

Memories are just dead men making trouble
—Gabriel Garcia Marquez

Al sits at his desk, watches headlights condense and evaporate in the murk outside. March, the hopeless season between the end of winter and the beginning of nothing. Spring breezes up from the sports section spread out in front of him, a banquet of names—Lakeland, Sarasota, Miami, Fort Myers— God, what he'd give to be there, feeling the broad plank of the bullpen bench splintering his butt, the low flame in his chest the first time he runs wind sprints, the teakettle wheeze of his breath. Instead it's days spent studying interest rates, answering questions about the tomato red Cadillac on the showroom floor for guys like Steve from Tonawanda who's *a big, big, fan, put her there, pal.* Wants to know who was the harder out, George Brett or Reggie? Wants to know how those bastards could have fired him, called it a retirement. *Like we were born yesterday, eh?* Al yanks off his jacket, shows Steve from Tonawanda his hands, the size of shovels, the hands that threw the best splitter in the business, one no-hitter, seven Series wins. Rolls the sleeves of his shirt, shows off his windup, watch this, his move to first, hell, yeah, he can still play. Plans to take it easy this summer, do some running, get rid of that twenty pounds he's put on. Hit the weight room, throw some BP over at the college. Come fall, get serious. Next winter, you watch, teams'll be banging on his door, begging him to come back. A million, million-five, maybe. Yeah, you watch.

Yes, I Have

Did I play baseball? Hell, pal, no one
calls it *base*ball, least of all
the guys that played the game.
Ballplayers—we say *ball*, or
The Show. Yeah, I been to The Show.
I seen the sights. Bartender? Same again
and one for my good friend here
John, sorry. Jim. . . Hey, you heard
the one about Joe and Marilyn?
She's hot off a plane after entertaining
the troops in Japan or Korea, I can't
remember. One of them long, skinny
countries tore up by war. Joe's
two years out of ball by then, got out
while he still had legs, or maybe he took
one look at the young Mantle, said, hey,
it's been real. Joe . . . he was a pretty
smart guy, not like Mays. You ever see film
of Willie that last year? Jesus. Like a drunk
fresh from a honky tonk on a Friday night. Makes
your heart hurt to look at him. Gehrig? Nah,
Lou got to die in private, yeah, I said *got to*. Not
like Mays, dying out there in front of God
and everyone, slower than an old dog
and he keeps on just because
he don't want to be forgot about.

So Marilyn. She's back from dancing
the hoochie coochie in a bathing suit
for a hundred million juiced up GIs and she
sashays up to DiMaggio and says, *oh Joe*
you never heard such cheering. And Joe, he's only

two years out of ball, did I tell you that
already? *Baseball.* Where else do they fire
your ass and call it retirement? Only a year
or two and already he's not Joe DiMaggio
anymore, not the Yankee Clipper, but
Mr. Marilyn Monroe, listening
to this little blond bimbo say, *oh Joe, you never heard
such cheering.* And Joe, who played in ten
World Series, TEN, he says to her,
Yes I have.

Jesus! *Yes I have.*

Hey, did you hear the one about
the ballplayer that played seventeen
seasons? No? Seventeen years and he's got
a dish rag for an arm, a scar the size of Rhode Island
across his shoulder, and fifty-two fucking bucks
in the bank BUT he finally gets why Gehrig
was the luckiest man on the face of the earth.
Because Lou got to die young and this ballplayer,
see, he's terrified, he's scared shitless he's going
to be old for a very long time.

Yeah, I played some ball.
Yes, I have.

The Math

Al never believed Boonie screwed
six-thousand women: 365 days, twenty years,
a woman a night, two, no way. It's all
in the wrists, Boonie would say, and only
catchers knew how. Sworn to secrecy
by the brotherhood, he would take it
to his grave and so he did. That long, brown box,
it's not really Boonie in there. Or else
it's all a big joke and any minute now the lid
will open and Boonie will laugh at them
for the grief that's slapped them all so serious.
One by one they get up and talk
about Boonie, what a guy he was
though nothing about the ladies
in deference to the wife. Someone says
it was her who found him floating
face down in the pool, *You can come out now,
Boonie*, immune to his pranks.
Only Al tries to explain what it's like
to be alive, to wake up to the sun
of another long day without
a ball game to play in.

North of Saginaw

North of Saginaw, south of somewhere
Al's never heard of,
a ball club in Michigan
needs pitchers. Pay stinks,
a couple hundred a week.
Seven-hour rides
in a school bus. A junkyard
for old men, their tattered arms;
smoke-throwing kids with no control,
the misfits with the jumpy
eyes of serial killers.
Still: grass, lights, applause, him
and the hitter.

In the Garden of Eden,
there were snakes.

City of Tonawanda Softball Championship

Two down, two out, two on in the ninth
when Sid Szymanski stands in at catcher,
sorry substitute for Larry whose sure
hands were summoned to a plumbing
emergency by his buzzing pager in the bottom
of the sixth. Still, the usual chatter
Hum baby, hey baby hum hey Sidder Sidder Sidder
though Zack's guys are mentally packing
bats in bags, unlacing shoes in order
to get away—fast—before the Panthers,
arrogant bastards, can gather at home plate
in a love knot of high fives and beer foam
and gloat. Strike two and Sid calls time,
steps out to take a couple of practice cuts
a la Barry Bonds, like him a big man,
all head and chest, and *Siddersiddersidder*
the car keys are out, that's all she wrote
when the pitcher gets cute with a breaking ball,
hanging it a nanosecond too long, time
enough for even fat sad Sid to get around
and give that pill a ride.

Rounding first, already red faced, a crowd
in his throat, Sid wants to believe
it's not the sludge of a million
French fries, but pleasure
more exquisite than the first breast
he touched one winter Sunday
while his dad in the den upstairs
cursed the Packers and Bart Starr, while his mom
chattered on the phone to her friend
Thelma about macaroni casserole

and menstrual cramps, Sid swallowed
hard and bookmarked his place
in *Our Country's History*, the page before
the Marines stormed the hill at Iwo Jima
and turned back the godless Japs, a high tide
clogging his chest as Alice Evans unfastened
the pearl buttons of her white blouse
and presented him with the wrapped gift
of her breasts, now second base and third
and the thicket of hand-slaps all the way
home where Sid hugs the center fielder
hurried and embarrassed the way men do,
oh, the moment, replayed again and again
over Labatt's at Zack's, the first pitcher
delivered by the great Zack himself
rumored to have been the swiftest,
niftiest shortstop on the Cardinal farm
but called to serve in Korea and after that
the closest he got to baseball was standing
next to Ted Williams at a Las Vegas urinal

Tomorrow Zack will make a place
for the trophy between dusty bottles
of Galliano and Kahlua while Sid
will field calls from customers complaining
about rising cable rates and too many queers
on TV, pretty much what he'll be doing
five years from now and ten when his wife
leaves a meatloaf in the freezer and runs off
with Larry the plumber and in twenty years,
when Zack's Bar is bulldozed
to make way for a Wal-Mart,
Sid will slump in a wheelchair
in a hallway littered with old men

mumbling and lost, wrapped
in the soft cloth of memory:
The arc of the white ball, a pearl
in the jewel box of twilight sky.

Nightcap

Saltines a can of soup a scotch or two or three or
more quenching the past replaying
on tape in his living room: Al
pitching his first game, Al
winning Game Seven, Al
lullabied by the announcer narrating
his no-hitter, the cheers of thousands
crowding his dream. He is young
again, he is strong
again, he is loved.
by so many.
Oh, listen
to how
he is loved.

Sarah Freligh was born and raised in Michigan and is a lifelong fan of the Detroit Tigers. She was the recipient of a Constance Saltonstall Foundation grant for poetry in 2006 and an Artist Residency Exchange Grant in 1997 from the New York Foundation for the Arts during which she completed work on a short story collection entitled *The Absence of Gravity* . A former sportswriter for the *Philadelphia Inquirer,* Sarah currently lives in Rochester, New York, where she's at work on a novel, *Half-Past Crazy.*

Printed in the United States
204736BV00001B/208-225/P

9 781933 456997